A true friend warms you by her presence, trusts you
with her secrets, remembers you in her prayers.

AUTHOR UNKNOWN

dinners we whisper secrets over.

The love of each one of you toward
one another grows ever greater.

THE BOOK OF 2 THESSALONIANS

11

is for

A Is for Always My Friend

Paintings by Gay Talbott Boassy

HARVEST HOUSE PUBLISHERS
EUGENE, OREGON

A Is for Always My Friend

Text Copyright © 2000 Harvest House Publishers
Eugene, Oregon 97402

ISBN 0-7369-0340-2

Artwork designs are reproduced under license from © Arts Uniq'®, Inc., Cookeville, TN and may not be reproduced without permission. For information regarding art prints featured in this book, please contact:

> Arts Uniq'
> P.O. Box 3085
> Cookeville, TN 38502
> 800-223-5020

Design and production by Garborg Design Works, Minneapolis, Minnesota

Harvest House Publishers has made every effort to trace the ownership of all poems and quotes. In the event of a question arising from the use of a poem or quote, we regret any error made and will be pleased to make the necessary correction in future editions of this book.

Scripture quotations are taken from the New American Standard Bible, © 1960, 1962, 1963, 1968, 1971, 1972, 1973, 1975, 1977 by The Lockman Foundation. Used by permission, and from The Living Bible, Copyright © 1971 owned by assignment by Illinois Bank N.A. (as trustee). Used by permission of Tyndale House Publishers, Inc., Wheaton, Illinois 60189. All rights reserved.

Printed in China

00 01 02 03 04 05 06 07 08 09 /PP/ 10 9 8 7 6 5 4 3 2 1

A friend is a
rare book of
which only one
copy is made.

AUTHOR UNKNOWN

By friendship you mean the greatest love,
the greatest usefulness,
the most open communication,
the noblest sufferings,
the severest truth,
the heartiest counsel,
and the greatest union of minds of which brave
men and women are capable.

JEREMY TAYLOR

A is

You are my friend and I hope you know that's true.
No matter what happens, I will stand by you.
I'll be there for you whenever you need,
To lend you a hand, to do a good deed.
So just call on me when you need me, my friend.
I will always be there, even to the end.

AUTHOR UNKNOWN

for always my friend.

My heart swelled with pride to
think you were my dearest friend.

LUCY MAUD MONTGOMERY
Anne of Green Gables

Encourage one
another day
after day.

THE BOOK OF HEBREWS

is for

6

The glory of friendship is not the outstretched hand, nor the kindly smile nor the joy of companionship; it is the spiritual inspiration that comes to one when he discovers that someone else believes in him and is willing to trust him.

RALPH WALDO EMERSON

believing in me.

A friend is someone who understands your past, believes in your future, and accepts you today just the way you are.

AUTHOR UNKNOWN

It isn't so much
what's on the table
that matters, as
what's on the chairs.

W.S. GILBERT
ON DINING WITH FRIENDS

is for

Few delights can equal the mere presence
of one whom we utterly trust.

GEORGE MACDONALD

If, out of time, I could pick a moment
And keep it shining, always new,
Of all the days that I have lived,
I'd pick the moment I met you.

AUTHOR UNKNOWN

your charming company.

D is for delicious

A friend is one who
strengthens you with
prayers, blesses you with
love, and encourages you
with hope.

AUTHOR UNKNOWN

everything you are to me.

Many friends will walk in
and out of your life, but
only true friends will leave
footprints on your heart.

ELEANOR ROOSEVELT

F is for

forgiving me over and over.

Constant use had not worn ragged
the fabric of their friendship.

DOROTHY PARKER

Every man should have a fair-sized cemetery
in which to bury the faults of his friends.

HENRY WARD BEECHER

is for going

True friendship
brings sunshine
to the shade,
and shade to
the sunshine.

THOMAS BURKE

It is not so much our friends'
help that helps us as the
confident knowledge that
they will help us.

EPICURUS

the distance in tough times.

It may be hard work
sometimes, but a friend's hand
and voice make it easy.

ANNA SEWELL
Black Beauty

Friendship is warmth in cold,
firm ground in a bog.

MILES FRANKLIN

The most I can do for my
friend is simply to be his friend.

HENRY DAVID THOREAU

A friend is what the heart
needs all the time.

HENRY VAN DYKE

A friend loves at all times.

THE BOOK OF PROVERBS

is for

Blessed is the influence
of one true, loving soul
upon another.

GEORGE ELIOT

20

We control fifty percent of a
relationship. We influence one
hundred percent of it.

BARBARA COLOROSE

helping me become a better person.

There is nothing better than the
encouragement of a good friend.

KATHARINE BUTLER HATHAWAY

 is for I

When we are grown we'll smile and say
We had no cares in childhood's day—
But we'll be wrong...'Twill not be true.
I've this much care...I care for you.

AUTHOR UNKNOWN

A hug lifts the spirit and deepens friendship.
It says: "You're a person of worth. You're a
friend and I care."

AUTHOR UNKNOWN

care for you, too.

J is for joyfully

Friendship is
one of the
sweetest
joys of life.

CHARLES SPURGEON

24

celebrating big days—and

Celebrate the happiness that friends
are always giving, making everyday
a holiday and celebrate just living!

AMANDA BRADLEY

little days—with me.

is for

Friends…they cherish each other's hopes. They are kind to each other's dreams.

HENRY DAVID THOREAU

26

kindness that never fails.

Kindness is love, but perhaps
greater than love…Kindness is good
will. Kindness says,
"I want you to be happy."

RANDOLPH RAY

One who knows how to show and
to accept kindness will be a friend
better than any possession.

SOPHOCLES

Kindness is the insignia of a loving heart.

AUTHOR UNKNOWN

Kindness is more than deeds. It is an attitude, an expression, a look, a touch. It is anything that lifts another person.

C. NEIL STRAIT

Life's simplest things are
love and kindly friends.

RIPLEY D. SAUNDERS

You have shown your last kindness
to be better than the first.

THE BOOK OF RUTH

How we laughed
and sang for joy.

THE BOOK OF PSALMS

is for

30

A good laugh makes
us better friends
with ourselves and
everybody around us.

ORISON SWETT MARDEN

the laughter we share.

M is for

more fun in everything because

I cannot even imagine where I would be today were it not for that handful of friends who have given me a heart full of joy. Friends make life a lot more fun.

CHARLES SWINDOLL

I do it with you.

For I have come to have much joy and comfort in your love.

THE BOOK OF PHILEMON

is for

There is a friend who sticks closer than a brother.

THE BOOK OF PROVERBS

O the world is wide and the world is grand,
And there's little or nothing new,
But its sweetest thing is the grip of the hand
Of the friend who's tried and true.

AUTHOR UNKNOWN

never walking away.

Be slow to fall into friendship, but when thou
art in continue firm and constant.

SOCRATES

is for

Precious gifts of friendship…knowing the heart of another, sharing one's heart with another.

AUTHOR UNKNOWN

A friend is one of those people who walk into our lives and find a home in our hearts.

AUTHOR UNKNOWN

opening your heart to me.

is for

Thus nature has no love for solitude, and always leans, as it were, on some support; and the sweetest support is found in the most intimate friendship.

CICERO

A friend listens with the heart.

AUTHOR UNKNOWN

patiently listening to

Thanks for the sympathies which ye have shown!
Thanks for each kindly word, each silent token,
That reaches me, when seeming most alone.
Friends are around us, though no word be spoken.

HENRY WADSWORTH LONGFELLOW

my troubles.

"Friendship," said Pooh, "is a very Comforting sort of Thing."

A.A. MILNE

Friendship is a cozy shelter from life's rainy days.

AUTHOR UNKNOWN

The love of our neighbor in all its
fullness simply means being able to say,
"What are you going through?"

SIMONE WEIL

The greatest healing therapy is
friendship and love.

HUBERT HUMPHREY

Oil and perfume make the heart glad, so
a man's counsel is sweet to his friend.

THE BOOK OF PROVERBS

is for

42

Yes, we are [friends] and I do like to pass the day with you in serious and inconsequential chatter. I wouldn't mind washing up beside you, dusting beside you, reading the back half of the paper while you read the front.

JEANETTE WINTERSON

quiet times together.

At first as they stumped along the path which edged the Hundred Acre Wood, they didn't say much to each other; but when they came to the stream, and had helped each other across the stepping stones, and were able to walk side by side again over the heather, they began to talk in a friendly way about this and that.

A.A. MILNE
Winnie-the-Pooh

R is for

My best friend
is the one who
brings out the
best in me.

HENRY FORD

There are high spots in all of our lives and most of them have come about through encouragement from someone else.

GEORGE M. ADAMS

reaching for the stars with me.

The greatest good you can do for another is not just to share your riches but to reveal to him his own.

BENJAMIN DISRAELI

S is for standing

Whether joyful or sorrowful, the heart needs a double, because a joy shared is doubled and a pain that is shared is divided.

RUCKETT

46

beside me through thick and thin.

Two are better than one because they have a
good return for their labor. For if either of them
falls, the one will lift up his companion.

THE BOOK OF ECCLESIASTES

T is for

Therefore…speak truth, each one
of you, with his neighbor, for we are
members of one another.

THE BOOK OF EPHESIANS

telling me the truth.

It is the best and truest friend who
honestly tells us the truth about ourselves
even when he knows we shall not like it.

R.C.H. LENSKI

is for

A friend is there when everyone else isn't,
believing when everyone else hasn't,
understanding when everyone else doesn't,
and loving when everyone else wasn't.

AUTHOR UNKNOWN

There can be no happiness equal to the
joy of finding a heart that understands.

VICTOR ROBINSON

understanding me so well.

V is for the

The best relationships…are built up like
a fine lacquer finish, with accumulated
layers made of many little acts of love.

GILBERT AND BRADSHAW

various ways you show

The smallest act of kindness is worth
more than the grandest intention.

AUTHOR UNKNOWN

you care.

W is for

Yes, we must ever be friends; and of all who
offer you friendship let me be ever the first,
the truest, the nearest and dearest!

HENRY WADSWORTH LONGFELLOW

wanting the best for
our friendship.

God has given each of you some special abilities;
be sure to use them to help each other, passing
on to others God's many kinds of blessings.

THE BOOK OF 1 PETER

We need old friends to help us grow old and new friends to help us stay young.

LETTY COLLIN POGREBIN

is for being eXactly

Thank you for giving me something
no one else could—yourself.

HEATHER LYNCH

God never loved me in so sweet a way before.
'Tis He alone who can such blessings send.
And when His love would new expressions find,
He brought thee to me and He said—"Behold a friend."

AUTHOR UNKNOWN

what I need in a friend.

I am glad that in the springtime
of life there were those who
planted flowers in my heart.

ROBERT LOUIS STEVENSON

There is no friend like an old friend
Who has shared our morning days,
No greeting like his welcome,
No homage like his praise.

OLIVER WENDELL HOLMES

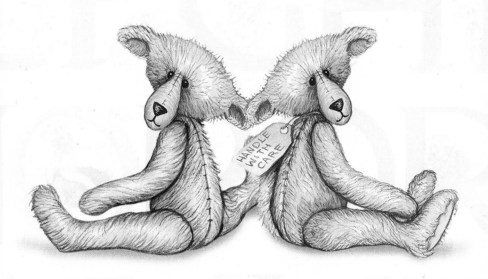

I do not cease giving thanks for you, while
making mention of you in my prayers.

THE BOOK OF EPHESIANS

The most wonderful of all things in life, I believe, is the discovery of another human being with whom one's relationship has a glowing depth, beauty, and joy as the years increase.

SIR HUGH WALPOLE

is for yesterday..

A friendship counting nearly forty years
is the finest kind of shade tree I know.

JAMES RUSSELL LOWELL

"Pooh, *promise* you won't forget about
me, ever. Not even when I'm a hundred."
Pooh thought for a little.
"How old shall I be then?"
"Ninety-nine."
Pooh nodded.
"I promise," he said.

A.A. MILNE
The House at Pooh Corner

and all our tomorrows.

is for zapping

Friendship is a strong and habitual inclination
in two persons to promote the good and
happiness of one another.

me back to reality every

"You have been my friends," replied Charlotte.
"That in itself is a tremendous thing."

E.B. WHITE
Charlotte's Web

now and then.

I'd like to be the sort of friend that you have been to me,
I'd like to be the help that you've been always glad to be;
I'd like to mean as much to you each minute of the day,
As you have meant, old friend of mine, to me along the way.

EDGAR A. GUEST